BUICK
1946-1960

Byron Olsen

Iconografix
PHOTO ARCHIVE SERIES

Iconografix
PO Box 446
Hudson, Wisconsin 54016 USA

Library of Congress Control Number: 2006926935

ISBN-13: 978-1-58388-178-1
ISBN-10: 1-58388-178-6

06 07 08 09 10 11 6 5 4 3 2 1

Printed in China

Cover and book design by Dan Perry

Cover photo- see page 74

BOOK PROPOSALS

Iconografix is a publishing company specializing in books for transportation enthusiasts. We publish in a number of different areas, including Automobiles, Auto Racing, Buses, Construction Equipment, Emergency Equipment, Farming Equipment, Railroads & Trucks. The Iconografix imprint is constantly growing and expanding into new subject areas.

Authors, editors, and knowledgeable enthusiasts in the field of transportation history are invited to contact the Editorial Department at Iconografix, Inc., PO Box 446, Hudson, WI 54016.

Acknowledgments

Most of the photographs in this book originally came from the company files of Buick Division of General Motors. Some came from the files of competitive auto manufacturers. All photos used are now the property of the National Automotive History Collection (NAHC) of the Detroit Public Library, Detroit, Michigan. The author would like to express his special thanks to the NAHC and Mark Patrick, Curator, for sharing these pieces of automobile history and helping to make this book possible.

Bibliography

The Buick, A Complete History, Terry B. Dunham and Lawrence R. Gustin, Automobile Quarterly Publications (1980)

Buick, The Postwar Years, Jan P. Norbye and Jim Dunne, Motorbooks International (1978)

Standard Catalog of American Cars 1946-75, 4th Edition, Ron Kowalke, Editor, Krause Publications (1997)

A Century of Automotive Style, Michael Lamm and Dave Hols, Lamm-Morada Publishing Co. (1996)

Buick sales literature from all years 1929 through 2000, Author's collection

The Production Figure Book for U.S. Cars, Jerry Heasley, Motorbooks International (1987)

The Complete U.S. Automobile Sales Literature Checklist 1946-2000, Kenneth Eisbrener, Iconografix (2005)

Introduction

The Buick Motor Company was formed in 1903 as a result of a reorganization of founder David Dunbar Buick's earlier efforts to build automobiles. The first automobiles bearing the Buick name were built about the same time. These first cars incorporated a unique valve arrangement that would become a trademark of all future Buicks and today is a design feature of virtually every automobile engine—overhead valves, or as Buick termed it for many years, "valve in head" design.

Buick was one of the first car builders to achieve volume production. The company was soon taken over by one of the great promotional geniuses of the early automobile industry, William Crapo Durant, who used Buick as the foundation for the formation of General Motors Corporation. In the early days of GM, Buick was the strongest component and was a material factor in propelling General Motors to a leadership position in the American auto industry. Along the way, some of the most esteemed names in automotive history worked at Buick—names such as Walter P. Chrysler and Charlie Nash.

Today, Buick is one of the oldest surviving divisions of General Motors, along with Cadillac. Through the years, Buick has usually been an industry leader. But there have been "downs" as well as "ups". One of the down times was in the early thirties in the depths of the Great Depression. Long established car companies were going broke right and left, and even some GM marques faltered and were retired like Oakland, Marquette, and Viking. There was even talk of scuttling Buick. Fortunately, another dynamic leader, Harlow Curtice, emerged at that time and proceeded to thoroughly revitalize and save Buick. He came from AC Spark Plug division and was bold, charismatic, and able. Curtice went on to become President of GM, but not before he had transformed Buick and spurred it into fourth place in sales by the forties, outselling all other American cars except the low-priced Fords, Chevrolets and Plymouths.

At the end of World War II in 1945, Buick had already been on a roll for a decade. It was poised to become a leader in the booming, car starved postwar U.S. economy. No new cars had been available for four years. Buick was ready with expanded production facilities and big, bold, new cars to meet the pent up demand. The year 1946 is where this book takes up the Buick story. Ahead lay years of phenomenal success for Buick in the late forties and early fifties culminating in achieving third place in the sales race by 1954. Unfortunately, disaster also lay ahead; by the end of the decade of the fifties, Buick's fortunes had plunged to seventh place in industry sales.

This book shows you the products that were responsible for Buick's successes and failures during the exciting years 1946 through 1960. They are all here, presented in sharp, original images that were recorded when the cars were new. There are no restored cars on these pages. Restorers and historians can rely on the images that follow to show the cars just as they were built.

This is not a history of Buick. There are many articles and several books that deal with that subject authoritatively and in depth. Notable among these writings is the definitive work "The Buick; a Complete History" by Terry Dunham and Lawrence Gustin, published by Automobile Quarterly Publications. Neither is this book an engineering study, except to note high points of engine development during the years covered. This book is a photo archive to give auto historians, Buick enthusiasts, collectors and restorers a more detailed view of what the Buicks of 1946 through 1960 looked like than can usually be found in more comprehensive corporate histories.

All of the photos in this book were taken at the time the cars shown were new. They were photographed by, or on behalf of, Buick Division, or by competitors trying to fathom the reasons for Buick's success. Most are from 8-inch by 10-inch negatives which afford detail and clarity not often found today. Most of the images are now owned by the National Automotive History Collection of the Detroit Public Library. I would like to express my appreciation to the NAHC for sharing their magnificent collection.

Today, as Buick enters its second century, it is still a major player in the industry, with a diverse product line. It has weathered many storms, and more challenges lie ahead as the now globalized auto industry becomes ever more fiercely competitive. We can hope that the resourcefulness and competitive spirit that has sustained Buick in the past will continue to do so in the future.

Byron Olsen
St. Paul, Minnesota, July 2006

This is the face Buick presented to a car hungry public in 1946 as peacetime prosperity returned after World War II. Typical of Buick in those years, it was bold, massive, and showed lots of chrome. The only change from the 1942 grille was the addition of two horizontal slots at the top.

This 1946 or '47 Super sedan, posed on a turntable, shows the extended front fenders that flowed all the way through to the rear fenders. Buick was the first production car to use this feature, and it was typical of Buick's style leadership. First seen on the 1942 Super and Roadmaster two-door models, it was extended to four-door models in 1946. There were virtually no other body changes from 1942.

Another view of a 1946-'48 Buick sedan, this one a 1948 Roadmaster. Supers and Roadmasters both used the GM "C" bodies, but the Road-master rode a 129-inch wheelbase, 5 inches longer than the Super. All of the extra length was ahead of the cowl, which made for a very long hood, necessary to accomodate the larger Roadmaster engine. Roadmasters were powered by a 320 cid 144 bhp engine, Supers and Specials by a 248 cid 110 bhp engine, both OHV straight eights.

For 1947, the only noticeable change was the addition of a heavy chrome frame around the grille bars. First introduced in 1942, the vertical bar grille became a Buick trademark until 1955. Shown here is a 1948 Super which used the 1947 grill without change (except for the dented grille on this car). The gun sight hood ornament seen here was another familiar Buick style feature.

In addition to four-door sedans, Supers and Roadmasters were offered as fastback two-doors (called Sedanets), convertibles, and station wagons, which Buick called Estate Wagons. This is a 1947 Super Sedanet. The Estate Wagon was available in the Super series from 1946 through 1948, but only in 1948 on the Roadmaster chassis.

The glamour leader of the late forties for Buick was the Roadmaster convertible. The script on the front fender identifying the Series was a change marking this as a 1948 model. Led by stylish cars like this one, Buick often held fourth place in sales, led only by the "low priced three"—Chevrolet, Ford and Plymouth. Dynaflow fully automatic transmission was first offered as an option on 1948 Roadmasters.

When car building resumed in 1946, Buick fully discontinued half the models it had offered in 1942. Betting correctly that it could sell everything it could build, Buick dropped most lower priced and low volume models in favor of the higher profit bigger cars. The only entry level Buicks left were the Special fastback two-door and four-door which used the GM "B" body. This is a 1947 Special four-door still using 1942 style fender trim and a body little changed since 1941.

The front compartment of a 1948 Roadmaster sedan showing the impressive dash, which certainly enhanced the car's appeal. The Super interior was similar but came without the chrome window frames and pleated door panels. Another characteristic Buick feature was the radio antenna mounted above the centerpost of the windshield. Using the knob above the rear view mirror, the antenna could be rotated up, or down to a parked position on the centerpost as shown here.

Buick built a reputation for big, upscale cars with roomy, luxurious interiors such as this 1948 Roadmaster. Notice the robe cord, the footrest, the courtesy light at the bottom of the seat, and the elaborate center-mounted smoking set complete with ashtray and cigarette lighter.

The rear of a 1946-'48 big Buick was equally unmistakable. This is a 1948 Super sedan looking characteristically massive with its bulky deck lid and big wraparound bumpers. The taillights included a separate pointed lens for the turn signals. In 1939, Buick was the first American car to introduce turn signals.

The 1949 models were the first Buicks to be completely redesigned since 1942. The '49 Buicks also introduced several "firsts" for Buick such as the portholes seen here on this Roadmaster sedan. Called "Venti-Ports", there were three on Supers and four on Roadmaster. That made it easier to spot Buick's top-line model. The Venti-Ports were functional in 1949, but soon became only decorative.

The new body on the 1949 Supers and Roadmasters was the GM "C" body, first introduced on 1948 Cadillacs and Olds 98s. The front fender line now flowed through to the rear fender at full height. The rear window was much wider and the windshield glass was now curved.

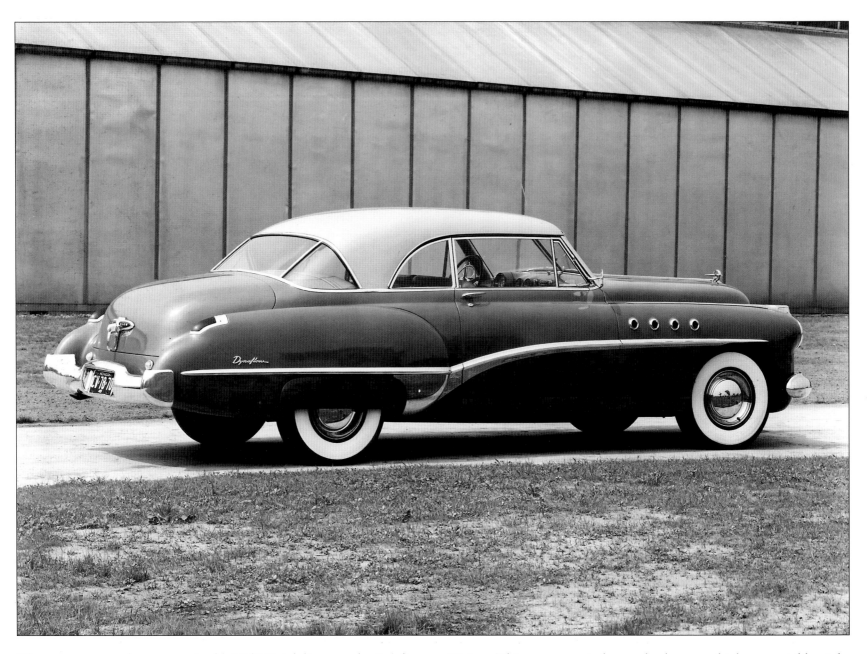

The most spectacular new car in the 1949 Buick line was the Roadmaster Riviera. This was an entirely new body type which was quickly nick-named "hardtop convertible" even though the top could not be lowered. The new body used convertible side windows, which left no door post standing when rolled down. The three-piece curved wraparound rear window further enhanced the feeling of convertible-like openness.

The Riviera frankly imitated the sporty lines of a real convertible as much as possible, while at the same time offering the safety of a fixed steel roof. Conceived by Buick people, the hardtop style was introduced first by Buick in mid-1949, followed a short time later by the Olds 98 Holiday and the Cadillac Coupe de Ville, both of which used the same body. Another first for the Riviera was Buicks' first use of the sweep-spear side chrome, which soon became a trademark style feature of most Buicks.

The convertible theme extended to interior trim. The Riviera used colorful leather and fabric like the convertibles and even used chrome roof bows to simulate a convertible top. Hydraulic power windows and Dynaflow drive were standard on the Riviera. The new body style was an instant hit and was soon imitated by most of the competition.

This 1949 Buick engine bay was typical of most '40s and '50s Buicks until the arrival of V8 engines in 1953. By 1949, Buick was the only American car that used overhead valve in-line eight cylinder engines. From 1941 through 1952, the hood could be lifted from either side or removed entirely without tools. For 1949, the Roadmaster used a 320 cid version rated at 150 bhp while the standard Super engine was 248 cid rated at 115 bhp (120 bhp with Dynaflow).

The Roadmasters rode a 126-inch wheelbase, five inches longer than the Supers. All of the extra length of the Roadmaster was in the hood to make room for the larger engine. After the Riviera was in introduced, Roadmaster convertibles like this one could also be ordered with the Riviera's sweepspear side chrome.

The 1949 dashboard was also changed significantly, although it still carried the Buick trademarks of massive dials and plenty of chrome. This is a Roadmaster sedan equipped with Dynaflow Drive, which also became optional on Supers in 1949.

The rear compartment of a 1949 Roadmaster sedan. Even the lower priced Supers offered the luxury of a folding center armrest. In addition to the body types shown, a fastback two-door sedan was also available in both Super and Roadmaster series.

The full-fendered 1949 design left very little room for woodwork on the sides of the Buick Wagons. Although the tailgate was still made of wood, the roof was now steel. This Roadmaster Estate wagon is living up to its name by being posed in front of a very lavish estate indeed. The Estate Wagon was also available as a Super.

Buick built an amazing total of over 21,000 Super convertibles like this one, which added to the record total of Buick production for the 1949 model year of 409,138 cars. Hydraulic power windows and seats were standard on both convertibles.

In mid-summer of 1949, production began on the first new Buick Special since 1941. At introduction, it was available only in fastback form as a two-door sedan, a two-door business coupe (no back seat), and a fastback four-door shown here. Initially, economy and low price were stressed, so exterior chrome trim was at a minimum. There was not even any bright trim around the rear window or windshield.

The grille of the new Special was its most striking feature, with grille teeth integrated with the bumper. This design was adopted by the entire Buick line in 1950, as was the wide hood and low front fenders. The VentiPorts were moved from the fenders to the hood sides.

Even though the new body was wider, in fastback form not much room was left in the trunk. The fastback body style was fading swiftly from popularity and would be gone from the Buick line early in 1951. Note that in this plainly trimmed 1949 1/2 Special, there is no trunk lining or floor mat.

The late '49 Specials turned out to be the predictors of the 1950 Buick lineup. The entire line, from Special to Roadmaster, was built with the same body with variations in length. Seen here is a 1950 Roadmaster sedanet looking just like the 1949 1/2 Special, except for much nicer trim and upholstery, and a five-inch longer wheelbase. This model, along with most other fastbacks, was discontinued early in the 1950 model run.

This is the 1950 Tourback bodystyle, seen here on a Roadmaster 126-inch wheelbase chassis. This body was also available as a Super or a Special on a five-inch shorter wheelbase. The abruptly chopped off rear door window treatment took some getting used to. Although the Super version sold many copies, the Roadmaster version was discontinued early in the model year.

The view over the dash of all 1950 Buicks looked much like this Roadmaster. Windshields on most models were now one piece, and dash paint was two-tone. The Super series was equipped with a new and improved straight eight engine, the F 263. It had a larger bore, larger 263 cid displacement, and more power—124 bhp (128 bhp with Dynaflow). The Specials continued to use the 248 cid engine which was rated at 115 bhp (122 bhp with Dynaflow). Roadmaster inched up to 152 bhp from 150.

The real star of the 1950 line was the Riviera sedan. It was available as a Roadmaster (seen here) and a Super. The Super Riviera sedan rode an exclusive 125-inch wheelbase, while the Roadmaster had its own gigantic 130-inch wheelbase chassis. Both wheelbases were five inches longer than the rest of their respective lines. These Riviera sedans were very popular and outsold all of the other four-door models. The toothy, and controversial, combination bumper/grille can be seen here. By the end of the 1950 model run, the toothy grille of the Buick had become a symbol of excess chrome on American cars. It would not be continued in 1951.

The Riviera sedans had extra leg room in the rear seat and an opening rear quarter window behind the rear door. The four "VentiPorts" on the hood mark this car as a Roadmaster, in case the extra length of the car was not obvious. Supers and Roadmasters were also available as Riviera two-door hardtops, convertibles and Estate wagons. The Special was offered in Tourback sedan and fastback sedanet versions.

The tufted seats and luxurious upholstery mark this as a Roadmaster, but the front compartment was essentially the same on all 1950 Buicks. When the 1950 models were announced, Buick cataloged no less than 19 models. Within a few months, 7 models had been dropped, yet Buick production reached a new high of 670,256 cars for the model year.

For 1951, the Buick grille reverted to a more restrained and traditional appearance. There was still plenty of chrome. The 1950 grille with its mouthful of teeth had made Buick the poster child for criticism of too much chrome on American cars. This is a Super Tourback sedan. Note that the parking/directional lights are mounted in the bumper guards.

Here is a side view of a 1951 Super Tourback sedan with its unusual squared off rear door window. Apparently the buying public was uncomfortable with the design, because it was discontinued after 10,000 1951 models had been built. A virtually identical 1951 Custom Special version was also announced, but never put into production. All told, Buick announced a total of twenty models at introduction time, but dropped four of them early in the production run.

Far more popular than the Tourback was the Riviera sedan. The 1951 Super Riviera model shown here sold over 90,000 cars. The Super Riviera four-door wheelbase remained 125 inches and power was unchanged at 124 bhp (128 bhp with Dynaflow). Other Supers used a 121.5-inch wheelbase.

Even though sales were low, the Estate wagon was continued in both the Super (seen here) and the Roadmaster lines. The Estate wagon bodies were built by the Ionia Body company and still used some real wood, even though most of the body structure was now steel.

This is the glamour queen of the 1951 Super series, the Model 56C convertible. Hydraulic power windows and seat were standard on Super and Roadmaster convertibles and Roadmaster Riviera hardtops. The sweepspear side trim was now used on most models.

The four VentiPorts on this Roadmaster Riviera sedan accentuate the extra length of its 130-inch wheelbase. Other Roadmaster models used a 126-inch wheelbase. The sweepspear side chrome, the massive bright metal window trim, and the chrome rocker trim ensured that Buick was still a contender for the title king of chrome.

Another contender for glamour queen of the 1951 Buick line was the Roadmaster Riviera two-door hardtop shown here. Notice the 1951 version of a riding lawn mower. The gunsight hood ornament was modified for 1951, and the hood medallion was surrounded by air inlets, to help "cool the engine compartment" according to the sales catalog.

The biggest change to the 1951 Buick lineup was the arrival of a new body for the Special. Shared with Oldsmobile, it was the first new General Motors "B" body since 1941. The new Special looked trimmer than its big brothers, yet was actually only an inch and one-half shorter than the Special it replaced, and rode the same 121.5-inch wheelbase.

This is the Deluxe Tourback Sedan. There were a wide variety of other body types available including a two-door Tourback sedan, a club coupe, a Riviera hardtop and, for the first time since 1942, a Special convertible. The new Special line helped Buick achieve its second best sales year ever—404,657, good for a solid fourth place sales ranking.

The new Special dashboard mounted some of the gauges in a different location than the Super and Roadmaster, yet the appearance of the front compartment was unmistakably Buick. Most Specials used one-piece windshields and Dynaflow was an extra cost option.

Few styling changes were made to the 1952 Buicks, in part because the '51s had sold so well. This 1952 Super Riviera sedan shows the shortened side sweepspear and the chrome fin added to the top of the rear fender. The trunk lid was squared off to increase luggage capacity. The sombrero style wheel covers were also new.

The Roadmaster, seen here in convertible form, had power raised to 170 bhp through one of the first uses in the industry of a four-barrel carburetor. Power steering was newly available as a Roadmaster option. Model year production was down to 303,745 due to the Korean war and a steel strike, still strong enough for Buick to retain fourth place in sales.

The Specials also had few changes for '52, since it had been heavily redesigned the year before. With the 1951 models, the Specials began using the improved F-263 engine as well as the Super series. This is a Tourback sedan with deluxe trim.

This is the 1952 Roadmaster Riviera sedan, Buick's largest and most luxurious model. There were colorful new interiors available this year, breaking away from the black and gray color schemes which had become a Buick sedan tradition. There were no changes from 1951 in models available throughout the Buick lines.

Buick entered its golden anniversary year in 1953 with a carryover body design now in its fourth year of production. Yet, clever restyling with a revised grille and a new combination headlamp/parking lamp gave the car a fresh look. This is a Roadmaster Riviera with optional wire wheel covers. The big news was under the hood.

This is a 1953 Roadmaster Riviera sedan. All Supers and Roadmasters now used the same wheelbases—125.5 inches on Riviera sedans and 121.5 on all other body types. The new compact V8 engine no longer required the five-inch longer wheelbase length to house the old Roadmaster straight eight.

Interiors were sharpened up with new, color coordinated fabrics, revised instrument panel finishes, and a new steering wheel. A total of 13 body types were available including four convertibles and two Estate wagons. This is a Roadmaster Riviera sedan.

The really big news for 1953 were new overhead valve V8 engines in both Supers and Roadmasters. Both Series used 322 cid engines, slightly larger in displacement than the previous Roadmaster straight eight. Yet the new engine weighed 180 pounds less. Buick adopted an alligator-type hood, finally abandoning the side opening style it had used since 1941. Twelve-volt electrical systems were also introduced on Supers and Roadmasters.

This Super convertible was almost indistinguishable from the Roadmaster version. Only three Venti-Ports instead of four, and a single chrome strip high on the rear fender distinguished the Supers on the outside. Supers were rated at 170 bhp while Roadmasters developed 188 bhp due to use of a four barrel carburetor.

The Estate wagon with genuine wood trim was still available in both Super (shown here) and Roadmaster form. The 1953 Buicks have come to be regarded as the last true "woody" wagons.

The roof and doors were steel, but the rear body posts and portions of the tailgate and side trim were still handcrafted wood. Buick Estate wagons were luxuriously trimmed with carpeted cargo areas. All 1953 Buicks had redesigned taillights as shown on this Super.

The new Skylark was the glamour queen of the 1953 line. It was based on the Roadmaster convertible, with cut down doors, a lower windshield, special upholstery and trim, and virtually every option. The Skylark foretold many future Buick design features such as full rear wheel openings, the dropped window sill line, and a slimmed down sweepspear. The wire wheels were genuine, the Venti-Ports were gone, and only 1,690 were built. Today, it is one of the most sought after post-war Buicks.

There were fewer changes in the 1953 Specials. This four-door Tourback sedan demonstrates the slightly squared off rear fender and deck line. There were three other Specials: a two-door sedan, a Riviera hardtop and a convertible.

This Special convertible shows off wire wheel covers, a popular 1953 option. The 1953 Special continued to use the F 263 valve in head straight eight engine. It would be the last car to use the engine type that had powered every Buick since 1931. Spurred by the new V8 engine in the other lines, Buick model year production rose to 488,765 cars, once again good for a solid fourth place in sales.

1954 was a year of spectacular change for Buick and the other users of the General Motors "B" and "C" bodies, Olds and Cadillac. GM styling trumped the industry with new panoramic windshields and dropped belt lines to create a dramatic and sporty new look. This Buick Super Riviera also shows how the sweepspear was slimmed down and the rear wheel cutouts on hardtops and convertibles opened up like the 53 Skylark. These changes showed off the optional wire wheels to advantage.

Roadmaster and Super sedans, like this Roadmaster, had a built-in sunvisor over the windshield and rain covers over the side windows. The heater air intake was relocated to the base of the windshield to avoid picking up exhaust fumes from other traffic.

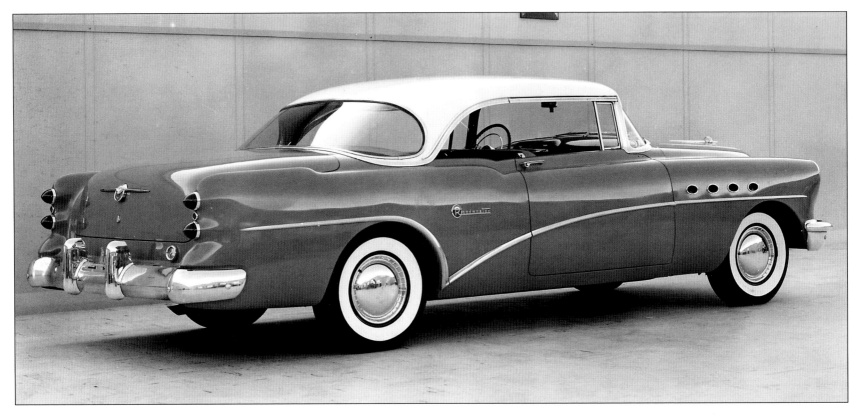

This Roadmaster Riviera view emphasizes the clean lines and abundant glass area of the new models. Wheelbase of all Supers and Roadmasters was increased to 127 inches and overall length to 216.8 inches. The Roadmaster V8 was now rated at 200 horsepower.

The only external difference between a 1954 Roadmaster sedan and a Super like this one was the number of Venti-Ports—still three on the Supers even though Supers used the same displacement engine and the same wheelbase. Supers were rated at 177 bhp, 182 bhp with Dynaflow.

The view through the windshield of this Super sedan gives some idea of the dramatic change in outlook brought by the new wraparound design. The instrument panel had some dramatic changes as well, with aircraft-type control levers.

This view of the rear seat in a Roadmaster Riviera demonstrates the feeling of openness brought about by the large rear window, dropped window sill line, and hardtop design.

The Specials used the equally redesigned "B" body, as shown by this Special Riviera. Specials had new V8 power for 1954, a smaller version of the Buick V8 with 264 cid and 143 bhp (150 bhp with Dynaflow). Note that the windshield post on this "B" body has a reverse angle. Windshield posts on the larger Roadmasters and Supers were vertical.

Another view of a Special Riviera showing the dropped belt line. For 1954, Buick brought back a Series name from the past, the Century. Like the pre-war Century, it used the Special body, but was powered by the Roadmaster engine. All 1954 Century models were identical in appearance to the Specials.

This is a new Special sedan. Wheelbase was 122 inches and overall length 206 inches. The Century sedan was identical in size and external appearance. Only Buick sedans and wagons continued to use fenders that covered the rear wheels.

Buick offered this handsome Estate wagon in both the Century and Special series. It was a significant break from previous Buick wagons. There was not a trace of woodwork left anywhere.

This rear view of a Special Estate wagon shows the transom-type upper tailgate. Public acceptance of the radically restyled 1954 Buick line was phenomenal. Model year production of 444,609 cars was sufficient to knock Plymouth out of third place in the sales race, unprecedented for a car as expensive as Buick.

After the sales success of the drastically redesigned 1954 models, Buick made only minor styling changes for 1955 in such items as headlights, taillights and other brightwork. The trademark Buick grille teeth were replaced with a textured mesh. Seen here are a 1955 Roadmaster sedan on the right, a Super Riviera in back, and a Special or Century convertible on the left.

The Super series was given the Roadmaster engine in 1955 which entitled the Super to four Venti-Ports. Power was increased to 236 bhp in all models except the Special, which was now rated at 188 bhp. Displacement remained 264 cid in the Specials and 322 cid in all other models.

This is a 1955 Roadmaster sedan (the Super looked almost identical). The massive new bumper, and bumper guards, made for a formidable frontal appearance. Wheelbase for both Super and Roadmaster remained 127 inches, while overall length was a garage challenging 216 inches.

The Century also gained a fourth Venti-Port in 1955 presumably because it used the Roadmaster engine. This is a Century two-door Riviera. At introduction, Buick offered a lineup of 15 models. During the model run, two four-door hardtops were added.

The Buick body design looked especially attractive in convertible form, seen here as a Century. The cut down window sill line gave them a rakish, European look. Buick offered four different convertibles in 1955 and built well over 20,000 of them.

The biggest news for Buick in 1955 was the introduction of an entirely new body style, the four-door hardtop. Called the four-door Riviera, the new body type was initially offered in the Century (seen here), and Special lines. The roof panels and doors were unique to this body, and considerable engineering effort was required to reinforce the body to replace the strength lost by removal of the center door post. The new body style was an immediate hit, and Buick built over 120,000 of them in 1955.

Another design challenge of the four-door hardtop was the complex engineering of the rear door window. When lowering, the window had to first back up to clear the overlapping front door glass, then drop into the door pocket nose first. Shown is the mechanism responsible for all of this monkey motion.

The Special Two-door sedan was the lowest priced car in the line, but still looked every inch a Buick. The Special was now the only Series with three port holes because of its smaller engine. For 1955, the rear wheel opening was fully cut out on the Special two-door sedans.

Unlike the two doors, the 1955 four-door post sedans retained covered rear wheels. This is a Special four door. The year turned out to be fantastic for Buick. Production of an incredible 738,814 cars was a new one year record and would not be exceeded for almost two decades. That total was almost ten percent of all cars built in the USA and ensured that Buick retained its newly won third place sales crown.

1955 was a year of bright colors and creative two-toning arrangements throughout the industry. This Special two-door Riviera shows one example with two colors used on the lower body. A common variation was to paint the roof to match the lower body color. It had been a great year, but 1955 would turn out to be a hard act for Buick to follow.

Changes for 1956 were minor, after the success of the 1955 models. Trim was cleaned up a bit, and the hood, grille, and headlight rims were given a forward thrusting "V" shape. This Roadmaster sedan shows how the sweepspear dip was raised, ahead of the rear wheel on all Road-masters. The setting is the Grand Hotel on Mackinac Island between upper and lower Michigan.

This two-door Roadmaster Riviera gives another view of the 1956 trim changes. The Super was identical in size and appearance, except for a deeper dip of the sweepspear.

Four-door Riviera hardtops were added to the Super and Roadmaster lines for 1956. Note the twin chrome strips on the deck of this Roadmaster Riviera. The wheelbase of both Series remained 127 inches and length 216 inches.

This 1956 Super sedan shows the deeper dip of the Super side trim. Power and engine size were the same in Century, Super and Roadmaster—322 cid and power raised to 255 bhp. Dual exhausts were new. All four-door sedans now had a fully cut out rear wheel opening.

Another Mackinac Island scene shows off the Super four-door Riviera. It was a strange place for automobile publicity photos as cars were not allowed on the Island. That is the reason for all of the horse drawn vehicles.

This view of a Roadmaster Riviera front compartment shows the completely redesigned instrument panel for 1956. The optional air conditioning was moved from the trunk to the dash. A dash-mounted air outlet can be seen on the right.

The Century continued to be the hottest performing Buick. It packed the Roadmaster 255 horsepower engine in the smaller "B" body. This is a two-door Riviera. There were a total of 19 Buick models in four Series available in 1956.

The Grand Hotel on Mackinac Island provides a lovely background for this glamorous Century convertible. Buick offered four convertibles in 1956 and sold over 20,000 of them. In addition, there were four each of two- and four-door hardtops, four sedans, two wagons and one two-door sedan.

Here is a 1956 Century four-door Riviera finished in a split two-tone color combination, a popular choice in '55 and '56. The four-door hardtop models handily outsold the post sedans in all four Buick Series for the first time.

This Special sedan shows off its newly opened up rear wheel cutout. For 1956, the fully exposed rear wheel style was extended to all Buicks. Industry sales were down somewhat for 1956, after the red hot sales of the previous year. Buick built 572,024 cars and easily held on to third place.

Even the lowest priced four-door Riviera, this Special, looked as classy as the more expensive Buicks. Only the three Venti-Ports gave it away. For 1956, the Special used the large displacement 322 cid Roadmaster engine rated at 220 bhp instead of 255, due to a lower compression ratio and a two-barrel carburetor.

This Special Estate wagon at the dock next to the passenger steamer "South American" captures some of the glamour of both forms of travel in 1956. Passenger service on the Great Lakes by the Chicago, Duluth & Georgian Bay steamships ceased years ago.

For 1957, there were entirely new bodies for all Buicks. This Roadmaster 75 two-door Riviera shows the new GM "C" body used on Road-masters and Supers. Most familiar Buick styling cues were continued, but in more accentuated form. The grille even returned to vertical bars. The bumper guards were moved outboard and resembled jet air intakes.

1957 Roadmasters were introduced with two chrome division bars through the rear window and connecting chrome strips on the roof and deck. There was a delete option for this feature which proved more popular. The division bars were a retro touch that was disliked by buyers.

As soon as it became evident that the division bars through the rear window were unpopular, Buick added the Roadmaster 75 model (seen here) with no bars and a more luxurious interior. All closed model 1957 Buicks (except some Specials) were now hardtops.

There were now just three Roadmaster and Super body types: four-door Riviera, two-door Riviera, and convertible. This convertible is a Roadmaster, still furnished with genuine leather upholstery in a choice of five color combinations. Note that the "C" body windshield post now has a reverse angle like the previous "B" bodies.

This is a 1957 Super four-door Riviera. It is outwardly almost identical to the Roadmaster, except for a few trim details. Wheelbase of 127.5 inches and overall length of 215 inches were also identical.

The all new GM "B" body used on the Century and Specials looked similar to the larger models, except for the angle of the rear window pillars. This is a Century two-door Riviera. Like the Specials, wheelbase was 122 inches and overall length 208.4 inches.

This is a 1957 Century, Buick's hottest and sportiest convertible. Engine size was increased to 364 cid in all models. Power was increased to 300 bhp (250 bhp in the Specials). That British Morgan sports car in the background is a sporting car of a very different character than the Buick.

This Century four-door Riviera shows how far the panoramic windshield now wrapped around to the sides of the new bodies. The side window sill line was also cut lower. The Special four-door Riviera looked almost identical.

The "B" body Buicks were also introduced with division bars through the rear windows. Buyers didn't like them any better than on the Road-masters. Unlike the Roadmasters, however, the bars on Specials and Centurys were part of the roof stamping and could not be deleted. This is a Special two-door Riviera.

The Special series had its sporty side, as demonstrated by this convertible at poolside. No one has explained what a car is doing on the pool deck. Use of an anamorphotic camera lens makes the car look longer and lower.

Post model Buicks now used the same roof panels and doors as the hardtops. It saved tooling money, but compromised the size of the door openings on the post models. In addition to the four-door Special shown here, there was a Special two-door and station wagon available with a center door post.

There was a new Estate Wagon available as a Century and as a Special. Seen here as a Special, it was a true hardtop, The Special version was also available in a door post version. The rear window was a wraparound lift up transom-type upper gate. The 1957 Buicks were not well received by the buying public, and model year production fell to 405,098 units, dropping Buick back to fourth place. But worse was yet to come.

The 1958 Buicks were heavily facelifted even though the body design was only one year old, because the 1957 models had not sold well. Traditional Buick styling cues were largely discarded, and brightwork was troweled on by the pound. The result was grossly overchromed at best, and garish and tasteless to many. The grille consisted of 160 individual chrome squares. This is a Roadmaster 75 four-door Riviera.

The chrome load from the rear was just as bad. This is another Roadmaster four-door Riviera displaying a slab of chrome on its rear flank. The division bars through the rear window were gone from all models. Also available in the Roadmaster Series were a two-door Riviera and a convertible. All Roadmaster and Supers had grown to 219 inches in overall length.

New for 1958 was the return of a name from Buick's past, the Limited. Distinguished by an eight-inch longer rear deck and different rear fender trim, the Limited was otherwise a Roadmaster in wheelbase (127.5 inches), power, and interior trim. It was available as a four-door Riviera shown here, a two-door Riviera and a convertible.

This view of a Limited two-door Riviera emphasizes the great length of the rear deck. Buick power remained the same as the previous year: 250 horsepower in the Specials and 300 bhp in everything else.

As in previous years, the Super looked very similar to the Roadmaster. New to the "C" body four doors was an operating rear quarter vent window. The only other Super body type available was a two-door Riviera. The Super convertible had been discontinued.

This is the "B" body Century four-door Riviera, distinguishable by its normally shaped rear window pillar. There is almost as much chrome as on the bigger Buicks. Century and Special wheelbase was unchanged at 122 inches although overall length grew slightly to 211.8 inches.

A Century convertible was still a good performer, and for 1958 had the brakes to go with performance. Buick introduced finned aluminum brake drums which immediately put Buick at the head of the pack in brake technology.

This 1958 Century Caballero Estate Wagon is probably equipped with optional air suspension. Cars so equipped would eventually settle down to their spring stops as the air leaked off. While it might permit racy poses for publicity photos such as this, air suspension was troublesome, unpopular, and dropped after one year. Other Century body types were a sedan and a two-door Riviera.

1958 Specials were available in the same choice of body styles as the previous year. This is a two-door Riviera. In traditional Buick fashion, it has almost as much brightwork as the top of the line Roadmaster. The public apparently didn't like all that chrome, either. Model year production plummeted to 285,089 units, less than 40 percent of the 1955 total.

Another view of a 1958 Buick hardtop Estate Wagon, this one a Special. The Special wagon was also available with sedan-type doors and a center door post. Hardtop wagons enjoyed a brief vogue starting in 1956, but were gone by the mid sixties. Buick dropped its hardtop style wagons after only two years.

A 1958 Special convertible posed in front of an unknown tourist destination. That is a Limited convertible in the background along with another '58 Buick. Through a combination of lowered air suspension, or use of an anamorphotic camera lens, this Special was made to appear even lower than it was.

After two disastrous years, all of the gains Buick Division had made in the early fifties had been lost. Consequently, another entirely new car was launched for the 1959 model year. It bore even less resemblance to traditional Buicks than had the 1958 models. Even the series names were new. Here is the top of the line for 1959, the Electra 225 four-door hardtop (six window version).

The overall design was refreshingly clean with lots of glass area and much less use of chrome. 1959 was, however, the year of the tailfin and Buick did its part. This is an Electra 225 four-door hardtop (four window version). Notice the unusual wraparound rear window. Electras used a new 126-inch wheelbase. Other Buicks (named Invicta and LeSabre) used a 123-inch wheelbase.

Of course, Buick had to follow a long standing automotive publicity tradition by posing lovely young women in swimsuits next to a convertible. In this case, it was the five year old Schultz triplets and a 1959 Electra 225 convertible. There were two other Buick convertibles: an Invicta and a LeSabre.

This rear view dramatically shows off all of the glass area in the two-door hardtops. Riding in the rear seat on a sunny day could be a warming experience. The fins are large, but the trim is very clean and neat. On the whole, the effect was a big improvement. Invicta and Electras got a new 401 cid engine with 325 horsepower. LeSabres used the previous year's Special engine of 364 cid and 250 horsepower.

Another view of a 1959 Buick two-door hardtop. This one is an Invicta, though they all looked very similar. The greenhouse and sides were also very clean and free from excess ornamentation.

Wagons were back for 1959, in both the Invicta and LeSabre lines. Bodies were larger and the hardtop style windows were gone. This is a LeSabre. Notice the compound curved windshield that not only wraps around the sides, but also up into the roof.

A view of the rear of an Estate Wagon, this one an Invicta. The rear window now rolled down into the tailgate instead of lifting like a transom. The new design was very low resulting in somewhat less comfortable seats, and in the wagon, somewhat less cargo height. But the growing size of traditional American cars was driving more and more people to buy compacts and imports.

A post-type sedan with a higher roof line was available as a LeSabre four-door sedan (shown here), a LeSabre two-door, and as Invicta and Electra four-doors. The clean cut new Buicks got good reviews from the motoring press, but generated only slightly better sales than the previous year of 285,089 cars.

After all the effort that had gone into designing the 1959 models proved not very successful, Buick designers had to try again by doing a facelift. As shown by this 1960 Electra four-door hardtop, sharp corners were rounded off, the grille was replaced, and even some stylized Venti-Ports were brought back. The Invicta and LeSabre had three and the Electra had four.

This Invicta two-door hardtop highlighted the heavy sculpturing done to the sides of the cars for 1960. Power for the Invicta and Electra again came from a 401 cid 325 bhp V8. The LeSabre still used the 364 cid 250 bhp engine, which could now be ordered in two optional forms: a regular gas version producing 235 bhp, and a performance version generating 300 horsepower.

This parasol roof four-door hardtop style was available in all three Buick Series. This is an Invicta. Few closed cars have ever had as much glass area.

This LeSabre Estate Wagon shared body and wheelbase with the Invicta wagon. All LeSabres and Invictas used a 123-inch wheelbase and an overall length of 218 inches. Electras had a 126-inch wheelbase and an overall length of either 221 or 226 inches, depending on body type.

A new addition to the Buick Estate Wagons for 1960 was a rear-facing third seat. Pioneered by Chrysler Corporation wagons in 1957, it took some time for GM to decide whether it was an idea worth adopting. There was a bumper-mounted step to aid rear entry.

This LeSabre two-door hardtop illustrates the expansive glass area that was common at this time in most car designs. Partly because of all this glass area factory installed air conditioning was becoming popular.

This car shows that Buicks could be ordered very plainly equipped. This is a LeSabre two-door post sedan, Buick's lowest priced car. The facelift of the '59 models didn't help; even fewer 1960 models were sold. The production total of 253,999 was the lowest for Buick since 1948. Buick had fallen back to seventh place in sales and rebuilding would take a long time and lots of effort.

Seeing a 1960 LeSabre four-door sedan in front of the Statue of Liberty with a happy young family should give everyone a sense of optimism for the future. Never mind that it is a composite photograph: one cannot park a car this close to Miss Liberty. But Buick nevertheless would bounce back in the decades ahead.

AUTOMOTIVE

RACING

BUSES

TRUCKS

More Great Titles From Iconografix

All Iconografix books are available from direct mail specialty book dealers and bookstores worldwide, or can be ordered from the publisher. For book trade and distribution information or to add your name to our mailing list and receive a **FREE CATALOG** contact:

Iconografix, Inc.
PO Box 446, Dept BK
Hudson, WI, 54016

Telephone: (715) 381-9755,
(800) 289-3504 (USA),
Fax: (715) 381-9756
info@iconografixinc.com
www.iconografixinc.com

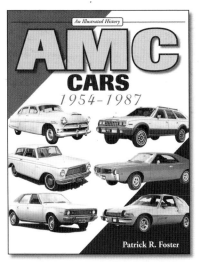

More great books from
Iconografix

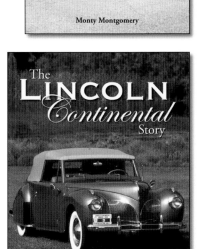

AMC Cars 1954-1987 An Illustrated History   ISBN 1-58388-112-3

Chevrolet Corvair Photo History   ISBN 1-58388-118-2

Pontiac's Greatest Decade 1959-1969: The Wide Track Era ISBN 1-58388-163-8

The Lincoln Continental Story from Zephyr to Mark II ISBN 1-58388-154-9

Chevrolet Station Wagons 1946-1966 Photo Archive ISBN 1-58388-069-0

Nash 1936-1957 Photo Archive   ISBN 1-58388-086-0

Oldsmobile 1946-1960 Photo Archive   ISBN 1-58388-168-9

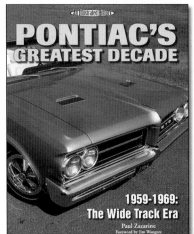

Iconografix, Inc.
P.O. Box 446, Dept BK,
Hudson, WI 54016
For a free catalog call: 1-800-289-3504
info@iconografixinc.com
www.iconografixinc.com

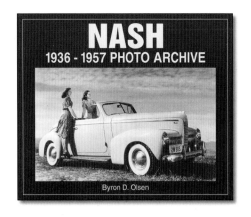

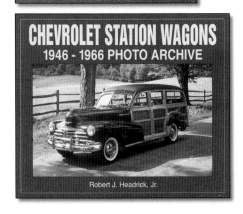

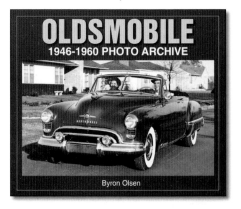